Hi! I'm **Snoop** – get to know me in **animals and you** every month. Now I'd like to know all about you...

This book belongs to

...... Dawn Masson ......

I am .....24..... years old

My school is

....

My best friend is

...... Alison and Coiln ......

~~Keso~~

Me

put your pic here!

My fave

tame animal ...... Rabbits ......

wild animal ...... Zebra+giraffe

tune ...... WestLife ......

book ...... Soaps ......

film ...... Disney ......

tv prog ...... Emmerdale ......

dvd ...... Hanwah Montana ......

game ...... O.S ......

My dream pet

put your dream pet's pic here!

Printed and Published by D. C. Thomson & Co., Ltd., 185 Fleet Street, London EC4A 2HS. ©D. C. Thomson & Co., Ltd., 2007

moggies OR doggies?

Some of these breed names are cats and some are dogs. Can you work out which are which and tick the correct boxes?

CORNISH REX
MOGGY ☐   DOGGY ☑

BURMILLA
MOGGY ☐
DOGGY ☐

HUSKY
MOGGY ☐
DOGGY ☐

POMERANIAN
MOGGY ☐   DOGGY ☐

CHOW CHOW
MOGGY ☐
DOGGY ☐

SALUKI
MOGGY ☐
DOGGY ☐

TORTOISESHELL
MOGGY ☑   DOGGY ☐

BALINESE
MOGGY ☐
DOGGY ☐

BOXER
MOGGY ☐
DOGGY ☐

NORWEGIAN FOREST
MOGGY ☐   DOGGY ☐

ANSWERS
doggy: husky, pomeranian, chow chow, saluki, boxer
moggy: cornish rex, burmilla, tortoiseshell, balinese, norwegian forest

5

pretty pics

happy families

A male rabbit is called a **buck** and a female rabbit is a **doe**. Does can have as many as 8 baby rabbits in a litter and these are called **kittens** or **kits**.
In the wild, rabbits live in large groups known as **herds** and sleep in underground **warrens**. Wild rabbits have many enemies including dogs, foxes, weasels and hawks, but domestic rabbits usually live to 8-12 years old if well cared for.

rabbits

Big ears, big eyes and short, fluffy tails - find out all about rabbits here!

take care

Rabbits are sensitive animals and like company, so they need a lot of care and attention. Nowadays, too many pet bunnies are left alone and neglected in outdoor hutches.
Outdoor hutches must be large enough for the rabbit to stand up in and should have a walk-in run and closed-in part for privacy. The best type of bedding is straw and this should be changed weekly or more often in summer.
Indoor rabbits need a quiet area where you can leave them at night or when no-one is around. Large dog cages with the plastic floor covered in straw are ideal. House bunnies can easily be trained to use a litter tray. However homes where bunnies are kept indoors have to be bunny-proofed - this means making sure there are no dangerous wires around for them to chew and no poisonous plants.

pet files

find out more about hamsters and guinea pigs.

Loveable, cuddly and cute.

hamsters and guinea pigs

pet facts

Hamsters and guinea pigs are both small rodents. Hamsters are quite new as pets as they were only brought to Britain from the Middle East in 1931. Guinea pigs have been here for centuries and originally came from South America. As both animals are very clean and don't smell they make perfect pets.

pig tales

Guinea pigs are not related to pigs and as they do not even look like pigs they may have got the name because of the grunting noises they make. They are also known as Cavies. Guinea pigs are very friendly and are happy to share their hutch with other guinea pigs.

pretty pics

© daj

DIZZY

life with Dizzy is never dull!

Hi, Mum. Hi, Dizzy!

Hi, Holly. What happened at school today?

I said I'd bake cookies or something for a candy stall.

There are some good recipes in the books in the kitchen.

So —

It'll need to be something easy as I'm not the best cook. Here's one. Fairy cakes!

I hope they work out, Dizzy. I want to raise lots of money for the dog and cat home.

Holly's brother, Jamie, came into the kitchen.

What are you making?

Fairy cakes for the school fair.

But the phone rang —

Oh, hi, Jane.

Much later —

Yeah, that skirt would look so cool with those shoes. Ssh, Dizzy, stop barking!

But —

But —

I'll just watch some TV . . . Oh, Dizzy!

They're ruined now!

What's all the noise about?

A little later —

Check out these furry cakes, Mum!

They look great. And what a clever idea to make them look like cats and dogs.

Well, Dizzy and Jamie helped a little too!

The End

13

Rainbow Girls

best friends

What will the mystical rainbow reveal about you and your friends?

Which would you rather watch?
High School Musical 3
Charlotte's Web 2
Happy Feet 1

At school you love
Sports and games 1
English 3
Art 2

What's your style?
Glittery 'n' girly 3
Funky and bright 2
Sassy and sporty 1

If you could have a celeb sister, who would you choose?
Hannah Montana 2
Raven Symone 3
Tracy Beaker 1

Pick a fave from these pop peeps.
Kelly Clarkson 2
Girls Aloud 3
McFly 1

Which of these would you rather do?
Shop till you drop 3
Visit an animal sanctuary 2
Go to a theme park 1

Your fave animal is
Dolphin 1
Puppy 2
Kitten 3

What to do -

work your way through the questions - each answer has a score at the end.

starting at the bottom of the rainbow, count along the number of spaces you score for each question. So if you pick **High School Musical** for the first question, count 3 spaces up the rainbow.

when you've counted along the rainbow for every question, see which colour you end up on. Now, check the Colour Chart to find how you rate!

now get your bezzie to do the same and find out about your friendship.

start

1 2 3 4 5 6

What would your dream bedroom look like?
Glitzy, pink and with the biggest wardrobe 3
Silver and full of the latest gadgets 1
Bright and comfy 2

Which TV show would you love to take part in?
Strictly Come Dancing 2
Dancing on Ice 1
X Factor 3

Imagine you're a huuuge star. What would you do with your cash?
Buy loadsa blingin' diamonds and jewels 3
Take all your pals on a fabulous holiday 1
Set up an animal rescue centre 2

12 13 14 15 16 17 18 19 20 21 22 23 24 25 26 27 28 29 30

Colour Chart

RED to ORANGE to YELLOW
You're full of fun and ready to try anything. You're a gold medal gossip and can't sit still. Bold and brave, you'll always take the dare.

GREEN to BLUE
You can seem a little quiet and shy, but your bezzies know what a fab friend you really are. Helpful, kind and trustworthy, you'd never blab a secret.

VIOLET to INDIGO
Hey, fashion kitten, you're glam and gorgeous! You love sparkles, shopping and girly sleepovers. Your friends rate you the Queen of Style!

Your Friendship
Work out your mate rate by counting the spaces between your finishing number and your bezzie's.

2 or less: Fab Friends! You two are totally tight - just like sisters. You share all your secrets and dreams.

3-6: Marvy Mates! You're cool pals but don't mind spending time on your own too. You know your friend is always there if you need her.

more than 6: excellent opposites! Opposites attract and you get along just great. Even if you do row you never stay cross with each other for long.

ALL ABOUT dolphins

We've fished around and found out these fab facts, all about dolphins - our fave animals ever!

Did you know that....?

they see and hear things deep underwater using echolocation. This means they send out a clicking sound and listen to the echo it makes. This then helps them to find other dolphins, objects and fish.

dolphins live together in groups called pods. When a couple of pods join together it becomes a herd.

the smallest species is the buffeo, found in the Amazon River. They rarely grow over 1 metre in length and 30 kilos in weight.

they have a thick layer of fat called blubber to protect them from cold temperatures. Dolphins that live in colder waters usually have thicker blubber than those that live in warmer waters.

dolphins talk to each other using lots of clicks, squeaks and whistles. Every dolphin has its own whistle to tell it apart from other dolphins - just like a human fingerprint!

ocean water is too salty for dolphins to drink. Luckily, dolphins don't need to drink much as they get water from the fish they eat.

one of the largest dolphins is the bottlenose dolphin. It can reach over 3 metres in length and weigh 200 kilos.

dolphins sleep by resting one side of their brain at a time. One side stays awake to control breathing. They only take short naps on the surface.

dolphins, unlike fish, can't breathe underwater. They have to come to the surface for air every few minutes. They breathe through blowholes on top of their heads.

dolphin
MAKE IT

Make this cute dolphin card for your bezzie - she'll love it!

You'll Need:
pencil
scissors
sticky fixers
dark blue, light blue and white card
wobbly eyes
tracing paper
glue

What to do

1. Trace over both parts of the dolphin template. Trace the BLUE template on to the dark blue card TWICE.

2. Trace the WHITE template on to the white card TWICE.

3. Cut out all the shapes.

18

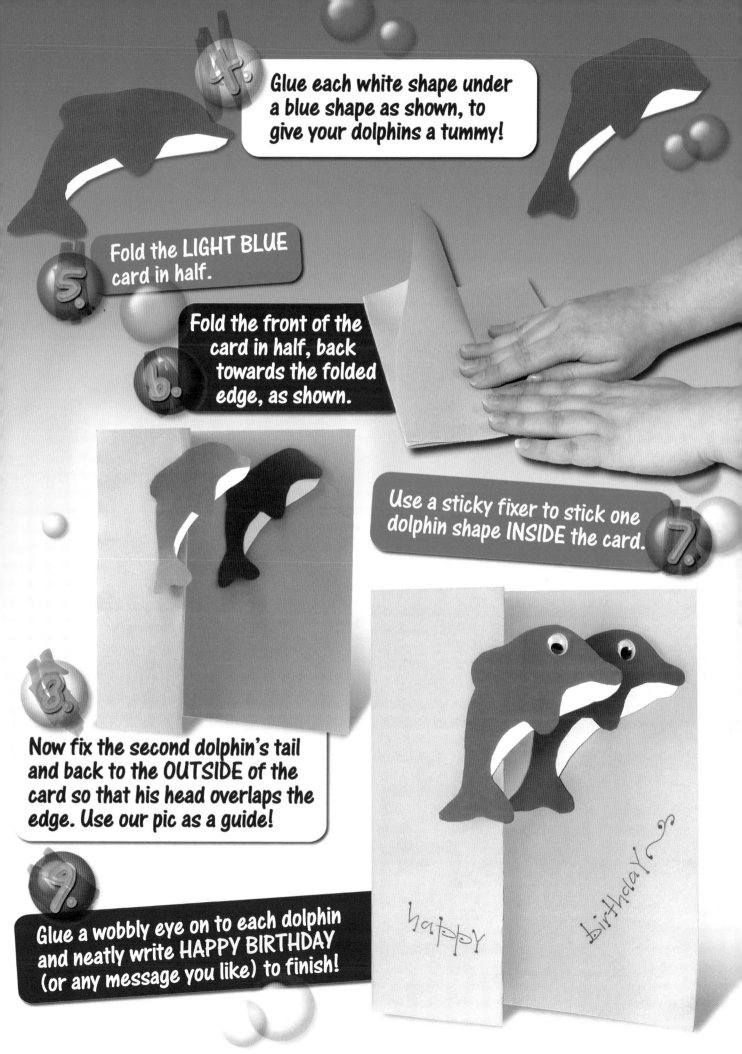

PET PUZZLES

Pens at the ready for these pet-tacular pet puzzles!

PARROT PAIR

Zara Parrot and her friend Tara may look the same, but there are four differences between them. Can you find them all?

NAME GAME

Unscramble the letters on the rubber bones to discover which doggy's toy it is.

ovrer

kipes

olegid

MATCH UP

Draw in lines to match the pet on the left with the word it matches on the right.

DOG   CURRY COMB
RABBIT   SCRATCHING POST
CAT   MIRROR
PONY   HUTCH
HAMSTER   RUBBER BONE
BUDGIE   EXERCISE WHEEL

A-MAZE-ING!

Which path should Molly Mouse take to get to the yummy piece of cheese?

a
b
c
d

PET SEARCH

Solve the clues then find the answers in the wordsquare.

1. Dog's home — KENNOL
2. Rabbits have 2 big ones — EARS
3. Young cats — KITTENS
4. A budgie can be this colour — BLUE
5. White dog with black spots — DALMATOAN
6. Guinea pigs don't have one — TAIL
7. The Tales of Peter — RABBIT
8. Holly's pet in Animals and You — BUZZS
9. Hamsters need a bottle of this — WATER
10. These make pets itch! — FLSAH
11. Outside goldfish live here — POND
12. Not a little Dane — GREATT
13. Libby's cat is called this — KIT
14. Budgies fly with these — WINGS

```
D I E R T R E T A W
I A S U A A E B R I
Z P L B L B N A G N
Z O E M T B B A R G
Y N N F A I Z E E S
F S N E T T I K T R
L W E F A N I N Z D
E I K E F L E A S N
E N R A B B T S N O
S G E R T A I L O P
```

HOW MANY

Poppy Pom-Pom's not happy. She's at the vet's waiting to be seen. Help her to pass the time by finding out how many 3 letter words or more you can make from

VETERINARIAN

1-10 Very good   **10+** Vet-tastic!

DOG DOs and DON'Ts!

Tick the box you think is correct.

1. Dogs wag their tails when they're happy. [do ✓] [don't]
2. Dogs sweat through their ears. [do ✓] [don't]
3. Dogs hear much better than us. [do ✓] [don't]
4. Dogs dream when they're asleep. [do ✓] [don't]

ANSWERS

african animals

Africa is home to many amazing animals. Here are some facts about just a few of them...

stripy

Zebras are most famous for their stripes but did you know that no two zebras have the same stripe pattern?

There are 3 different species of zebra and all live in Africa.

The Grevy's zebra and mountain zebra are more endangered than the common Burchell's zebra.

Zebras are members of the horse family and have hooved feet and a mane.

A baby zebra is called a foal. A foal can stand within 15 minutes of being born.

wrinkly

Elephants are the largest mammals living on land.

The African elephant is different from the Asian elephant in a few ways - the African elephant has larger ears which it flaps to keep cool. Male Asian elephants have tusks but both male and female African elephants have tusks.

They talk to each other using very low growls which we can hardly hear.

An elephant's trunk is so strong it can rip branches from trees but it is also so delicate it can pick up tiny berries from the ground.

hairy

- Gorillas are the largest of the primates (the monkey family).

- Older males are called Silverbacks as they have lots of silvery hair on their backs.

- Gorillas eat plants, leaves, buds, flowers and sometimes insects.

- They build a nest to sleep in each night using branches and leaves high up in the trees.

- Large males are so heavy that they spend most of their time on the ground and even sleep there.

- Gorillas are one of the most endangered animals on the planet.

spotty

- The cheetah is the world's fastest land mammal and can run as fast as 60 miles per hour - that's a mile a minute!

- They have solid spots on their fur and black marks running from the corner of each eye.

- Unlike other big cats cheetahs hunt during the day.

- Also unlike other big cats (and house cats!), they cannot put their claws away. They use them for gripping the ground as they run.

- Unfortunately, cheetahs are very endangered.

big cat rescue!

Born Free have saved three beautiful lions from a horrible cage in France and given them a new life in their big cat sanctuary, Shamwari, in South Africa.

Nalla

Shada

Djunka

france

The cats had been living in a tiny, rusty trailer in France as part of a circus for NINE years! Each cat only had an area of 2m by 2m to turn around.

The first thing Born Free had to do was give the lions some medicine to make them very sleepy so they could be taken from their trailer and checked over by a vet. The cats were very thin and poor Nalla and Djunka had lost a lot of weight which was a worry, but luckily they were fit enough to travel. This is a very sleepy Nalla being checked over by the vet.

airport

Next, the lions were loaded into travelling crates to begin their long journey from France to Africa. They travelled by air, ferry and road. People were there to check that they had enough water and were okay during this trip.

africa

The moment of freedom arrived for the lions. First Nalla was let out of her crate, then Shada and finally Djunka. Each cat's crate was opened in the enclosure they would be living in. Nalla and Shada jumped out as soon as their crates were opened and started to have a look round their big enclosures.

Shamwari

The lions seemed to be very interested in the tall grass as they were used to the bars of their trailer.

The cats are now happily living in their huge enclosures. Djunka loves to run, something he couldn't do before. Shada likes to hide in the tall grasses and Nalla is getting special care and loves the warm sunshine. They are much happier lions who can now have the freedom to be almost wild.

Shada

Nalla

Djunka

You can adopt all three lions for just £2 a month! Log onto www.bornfree.org.uk

25

Stars in your Eyes!

Are you gonna be famous some day? Follow our fun flow and find out which cool career would suit you best!

Start
Do you like being the centre of attention?

All you want for your birthday is an iPod!

Your room's full of McFly posters!

Do you sing in the shower?

You want to learn to play guitar.

You can be a bit bossy.

You write stories in your spare time.

You hate talking in front of people.

You tell the best sleepover stories!

English is your fave subject.

You're gonna be a total rock chick like Kelly Clarkson! Music's definitely the career for you.

You've got tons of imagination and you'd be a great writer, just like Cathy Cassidy!

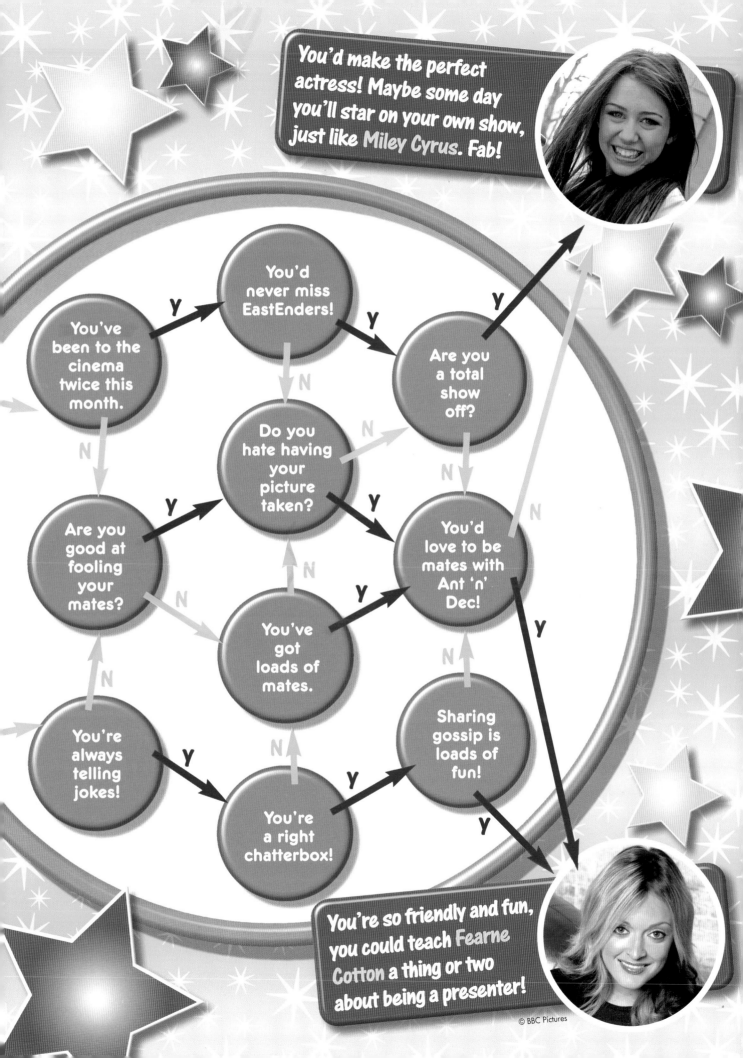

You'd make the perfect actress! Maybe some day you'll star on your own show, just like Miley Cyrus. Fab!

You've been to the cinema twice this month.

Y

You'd never miss EastEnders!

Y

Are you a total show off?

N

Do you hate having your picture taken?

N

N

Y

You'd love to be mates with Ant 'n' Dec!

N

Are you good at fooling your mates?

Y

N

You've got loads of mates.

Y

N

N

You're always telling jokes!

Y

You're a right chatterbox!

Y

Sharing gossip is loads of fun!

Y

Y

You're so friendly and fun, you could teach Fearne Cotton a thing or two about being a presenter!

© BBC Pictures

I wanna be... a Vet!

Maya really wants to be a vet, so we took her along to a PDSA PetAid hospital to see how it's done!

First, Stephan, the vet, showed Maya around the PetAid hospital.

This is where we first examine sick and injured pets...

Time for some work!

You'll have to put your scrubs on so you can help me.

This is where Jet will have to sit for his x-ray.

You're being really good, Jet.

Nearly finished...

We have to check all the equipment before it gets cleaned.

What do you think, Kai?

Maya reads all about PDSA's Pet Protectors Club

28

Being a vet's a lot of work....

You'll have to study really hard!

These are heavy!

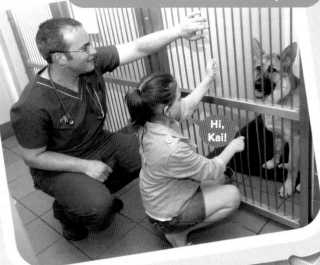

But you get to help gorgeous animals like Kai, the German Shepherd!

Hi, Kai!

Time to check the x-ray!

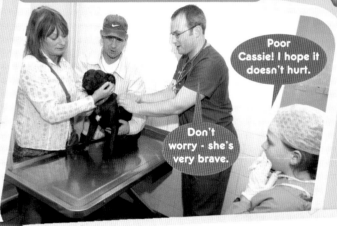

Hmmmm....

Next, Cassie needs to be vaccinated.

Poor Cassie! I hope it doesn't hurt.

Don't worry - she's very brave.

Time to say goodbye!

I hope you had fun today, Maya.

Yes, thanks! Working with animals is great!

win! pdsa pet protectors

PDSA Pet Protectors is a great way to help sick and injured animals! Yearly membership costs £8 and includes a free gift, a Pet Protectors badge, a membership card and six issues of the club magazine, Animal Antics. Visit www.youngpdsa.org.uk for more info on PDSA and the Pet Protectors Club.

Would you like a year's membership to the Pet Protectors Club? To be in with a chance of winning simply write your name, age, address and parent/guardian's signature on a card or stuck down envelope and send to: Pet Protectors, Animals and You Annual 2008, P.O. Box 305, London NW1 1TX.

The first entry out of the bag wins the prize. The Editor's decision is final and no correspondence will be entered into. This is a joint promotion between Animals and You and PDSA who are supplying the prize.

bear search!

Hunt for all these bear words in the wordsquare. Words can read up, down, forwards, backwards or diagonally. One of the words is often mistaken for a type of bear. Do you know which one?

- GRIZZLY
- BROWN
- POLAR
- RED PANDA
- PANDA
- BLACK
- WHITE
- PATCH
- GIANT CAT BEAR
- KOALA
- FOOD
- LEAVES
- BERRIES
- FRUIT
- SALMON
- BAMBOO
- SHOOTS
- ROOTS
- FISH
- HONEY
- MEAT
- HIBERNATE
- CLAWS
- FUR
- SNOUT
- GROWL
- GRUNTS
- CUBS
- ENDANGERED
- POWERFUL
- HABITATS
- MOUNTAINS
- FORESTS
- CHINA
- AMERICA
- ARCTIC

E	N	W	O	R	B	A	C	T	U	O	N	S	O	T	L
G	N	O	M	L	A	S	B	U	C	S	R	N	S	I	E
R	E	D	P	H	T	C	P	A	T	E	J	I	T	U	A
O	D	I	G	S	H	R	O	T	D	M	T	A	O	R	V
W	H	T	E	I	U	B	N	P	A	A	S	T	O	F	E
L	P	R	N	F	A	G	A	W	E	L	K	N	H	C	S
U	O	A	R	U	T	N	E	M	A	C	A	U	S	I	G
F	O	O	D	F	D	X	T	E	B	A	B	O	C	T	K
R	H	C	T	A	P	S	I	C	L	O	E	M	K	C	Y
E	M	O	D	O	N	Y	H	T	A	Y	O	T	A	R	S
W	S	N	L	A	L	M	W	B	E	T	N	L	B	A	W
O	A	A	R	Z	E	T	A	N	R	E	B	I	H	D	A
P	R	F	Z	A	F	K	O	A	C	I	R	E	M	A	L
R	U	I	T	S	O	H	S	T	A	T	I	B	A	H	C
O	R	C	B	E	R	R	I	E	S	S	T	O	O	R	F
G	R	U	N	T	S	D	E	R	E	G	N	A	D	N	E

© Purestock

ANSWER:
Koala is not a bear – it's a marsupial which means it carries its young in a pouch.

30

Panda Posers

Aaw! Isn't this panda sweet? But other than being cute and cuddly, what do you know about pandas? Here's some info.....

Pandas are black and white bears that live in the cold mountain bamboo forests of China. The Chinese name for a giant panda is da xiong mao - meaning giant cat bear. Their fave food is bamboo shoots and, as it's their only food, they have to eat lots to get enough goodness.

Sadly, many of the bamboo forests are being cleared, leaving less bamboo for the pandas to eat, so our furry friends are becoming endangered.

Pandas have 42 teeth and spend around 12 hours each day eating and the rest sleeping. They are shy, quiet creatures that like to live alone.

Now try our fun PANDA PUZZLERS... Tick the correct answer

1. What is a panda's fave food?
a) berries ☐
b) bamboo ☐
c) insects ☐

2. Which country is the home of pandas?
c) Spain ☐
b) China ☐
a) India ☐

3. How many teeth do pandas have?
c) 32 ☐
a) 52 ☐
b) 42 ☐

4. What colours are giant pandas?
a) yellow and brown ☐
c) grey and brown ☐
b) black and white ☐

5. How many hours each day do pandas sleep?
c) 8 ☐
b) 12 ☐
a) 10 ☐

Now score 3 points for every *b* that you ticked. How did you *bear* up?

12 - 15	PANDA-TASTIC!
6 - 11	FURRY GOOD
0 - 5	PANDA PUZZLED

© Purestock

a Kitten

Katie Taylor was feeling really sad. Her cat, Snax, had just died.

I miss you so much, Snax.

Snax won't be needing these any more, but I can't throw them out.

It's Snax!

It's just a cat that looks like Snax, Katie.

I know, Mum. I just got such a surprise when I saw her.

Hello, girl. You're different from Snax when I see you close up. You're smaller and fluffier.

Oh! I must have scared her. I hope she comes back.

for Katie

The next day —

I don't believe it! Mum!

Look, Mum! Out in the garden!

The following day —

She's there again!

I'm going to say hello to that cat.

Do you think she's a stray, Mum?

Well, she's not wearing a collar with identification . . .

When the cat returned —

Would you like some tuna? Snax loved that!

But, as Mum read the local paper —

I don't believe it!

What is it, Mum?

There's a photo of the cat. Her owner is looking for her.

Oh, no! It's like losing Snax all over again!

It's my Poppy! Thank you so much for bringing her back to me. Come in.

I was so worried about Poppy. You see she's expecting kittens very soon.

Mum, would that be okay? Can I have a kitten?

Of course, Katie! The house hasn't been the same without a cat.

Oh, Mum! It's like Poppy was meant to come into our garden and find us!

The end

cheeky chimps!

Chimpanzees...

... are very clever apes
... are closely related to humans
... have very long arms and lots of black hair
... love to play and swing through tree branches

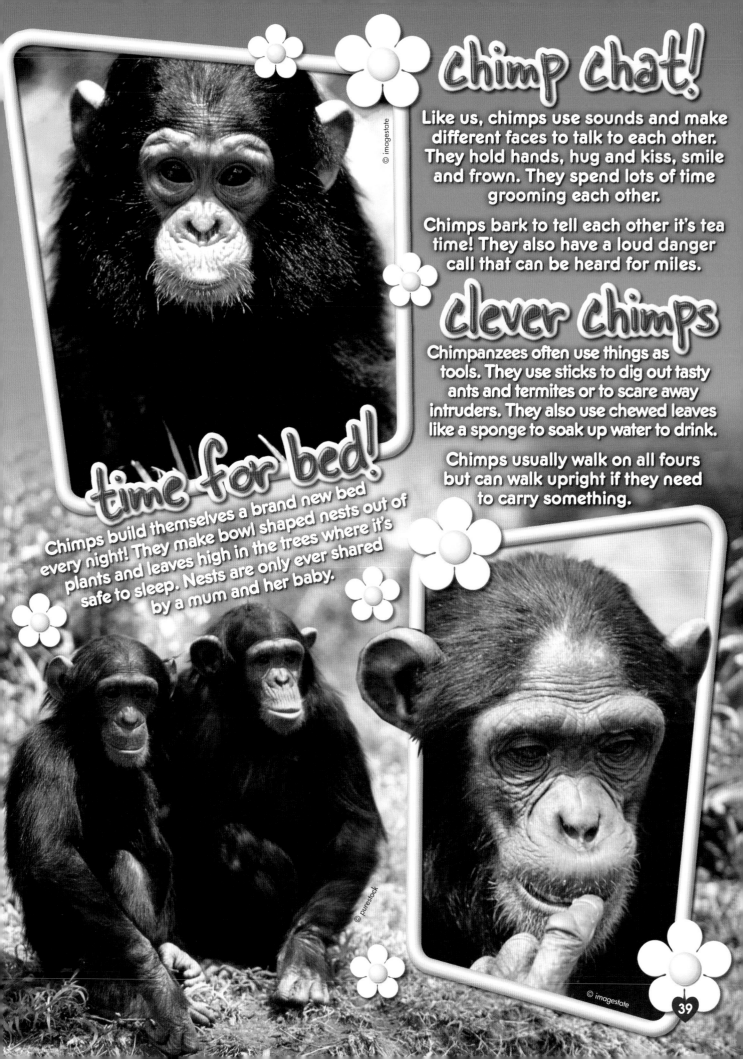

chimp chat!

Like us, chimps use sounds and make different faces to talk to each other. They hold hands, hug and kiss, smile and frown. They spend lots of time grooming each other.

Chimps bark to tell each other it's tea time! They also have a loud danger call that can be heard for miles.

clever chimps

Chimpanzees often use things as tools. They use sticks to dig out tasty ants and termites or to scare away intruders. They also use chewed leaves like a sponge to soak up water to drink.

Chimps usually walk on all fours but can walk upright if they need to carry something.

time for bed!

Chimps build themselves a brand new bed every night! They make bowl shaped nests out of plants and leaves high in the trees where it's safe to sleep. Nests are only ever shared by a mum and her baby.

© imagestate

© purestock

© imagestate

39

adorable orangutans!

Orangutans...

... can't swim

... have very very long arms

... live in Borneo and Sumatra

... are covered in long orange hair!

... are the second largest of all the apes - about 2/3 size of a gorilla

© brandX

high life

Orangutans live in high treetops and are the largest tree-living animals. They prefer to live alone and move through the forest by swinging from branch to branch. Their fave food is fruit.

Like chimps, orangutans are very clever and also build themselves a bed each night. Sometimes they use big leaves as umbrellas!

© purestock

baby love!

Orangutans make very good mums. The babies snuggle close and cling to Mum's hair as they swing through the trees. They love to kiss and cuddle each other. A baby will stay with its mum for 6 - 7 years!

© purestock

orangutans in danger!

Orangutans are very rare and hardly any are left in the wild. Their biggest enemy is man. The forests where orangutans live are being cut down and sometimes babies are stolen to be sold as pets.

© brandX

There are less Sumatran orangutans left than Bornean ones. Log on to

www.orangutan.org.uk

to find out more.

41

penguin puzzles

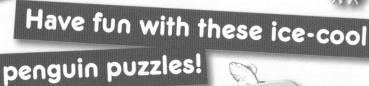

Have fun with these ice-cool penguin puzzles!

HOP TO IT!
Penny's lost one of her ice skates. Hop her through the maze to find it.

name game

Unscramble these letters to find out the name of Penny's favourite flower.

R O

P W O

N

S D

YUMMY!

Using this secret number code, find out what Penny loves to eat.

9 = A   2 = C   7 = D   4 = F   8 = H
1 = I   5 = N   3 = P   6 = S

4168   957   28136

BRR!

It's cold in the Antarctic and lots of words begin with either SNOW or ICE.

This list of words can make other words when *snow* or *ice* is put in front of them. Place them in the column you think is right.

AGE, AXE, BAG, BALL, BERG, BOARD, BOX, CREAM, DRIFT, FALL, FLAKE, FLOE, GOOSE, HOCKEY, LEOPARD, LOLLY, MAN, PACK, PICK, PLOUGH, SHOE, SKATE, STORM, WHITE.

SNOW	ICE

PICK-A-PENGUIN

Place these types of penguins into the correct squares on the grid and the biggest breed of penguin will appear in the shaded column.

ADELIE   MACARONI
CHINSTRAP   ROCKHOPPER
GENTOO   ROYAL
HUMBOLDT

A D E L I E
h u m b o l d t
R O C K h O P P e r
G E n T O O
M A C A R O N I
R O Y A L
C h i n s t r a p

PENGUIN PAIR

Penny and her penguin pals love ice skating. They may look the same, but only two of them are identical. Can you find the penguin pair?

a   b   c   d

PENGUIN PATTER

Penny is so excited about going ice skating that all her words are joined together. Can you work out what she's saying?

MEETYOUATTHEICERINKATTWOO'CLOCK

There are ten tiny tiddlers just like this hidden on these pages. Can you find them all?

answers:

PENGUIN PAIR - a & c; NAME GAME - Snowdrop; BRR! SNOW - ball, board, drift, fall, flake, goose, leopard, man, plough, shoe, storm, white. ICE - age, axe, bag, berg, box, cream, floe, hockey, lolly, pack, pick, skate. YUMMY - Fish and chips. PICK-A-PENGUIN - Adelie, Humboldt, Rockhopper, Gentoo, Macaroni, Royal, Chinstrap - Emperor. PENGUIN PATTER - Meet you at the ice rink at two o' clock.

43

Millie at WOOD GREEN

Millie and her mum are visiting Wood Green Animal Shelter. There are hundreds of animals looking for new homes. The rehoming team will help them find the perfect pet.

Millie

Holly

At the Ranch, Millie meets Holly - she's so friendly! Holly was sad living on her own, so she came here to find a new family. Holly needs to live somewhere where she can have friends.

DJ

Nosy little DJ comes over to see what's going on. He was brought up in a house - just like a dog! When he got too big, he had to come to Wood Green too. He loves cuddles and attention.

Bella

Bella is a beautiful, sweet and gentle horse. She's too old to be ridden now, but would make a lovely friend for another horse or pony. Bella's too big for Millie's garden!

Bunnies

Millie loves the fluffy bunnies. Thousands of rabbits are abandoned or left alone in their hutches every year - some without food! People just get bored looking after them.

Alfie

Alfie is sooo cuddly, but he needs a special diet to help him lose weight. He's lost lots already, but it'll still be a while before he can go to a new home.

Archie

Archie the lurcher is still only a 20 week old puppy! He has lots of fun playing with Millie, but he's too full of bouncy beans to live in their small house.

Fluffball

The giggly guinea pigs are enjoying the sunshine. Look at Fluffball - he has crazy curly hair!

Guinea pigs like company, so Wood Green always rehome them in pairs. Fluffball has to wait till a girlfriend arrives for him. He'll also have an operation to stop lots of baby guineas being born.

Kittens

These little kittens are super sweet! Millie would love a cat, so one of these cuties is the perfect pet for her. Only problem now is which one to choose!

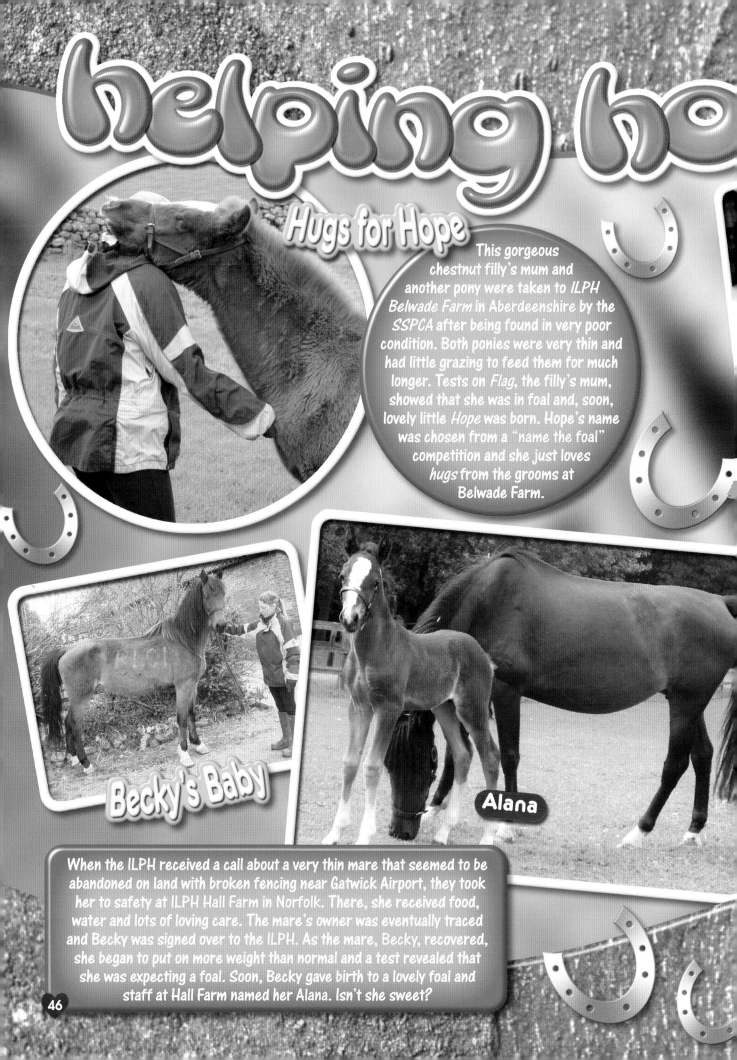

helping ha

Hugs for Hope

This gorgeous chestnut filly's mum and another pony were taken to *ILPH Belwade Farm* in Aberdeenshire by the *SSPCA* after being found in very poor condition. Both ponies were very thin and had little grazing to feed them for much longer. Tests on *Flag*, the filly's mum, showed that she was in foal and, soon, lovely little *Hope* was born. Hope's name was chosen from a "name the foal" competition and she just loves *hugs* from the grooms at Belwade Farm.

Becky's Baby

Alana

When the ILPH received a call about a very thin mare that seemed to be abandoned on land with broken fencing near Gatwick Airport, they took her to safety at ILPH Hall Farm in Norfolk. There, she received food, water and lots of loving care. The mare's owner was eventually traced and Becky was signed over to the ILPH. As the mare, Becky, recovered, she began to put on more weight than normal and a test revealed that she was expecting a foal. Soon, Becky gave birth to a lovely foal and staff at Hall Farm named her Alana. Isn't she sweet?

...ses!

Aaw! Here are some sad tales with happy endings – thanks to ILPH (International League for the Protection of Horses)! The ILPH cares for horses that have been badly treated or abandoned and then finds them new homes whenever possible. Take a look at the stories here →

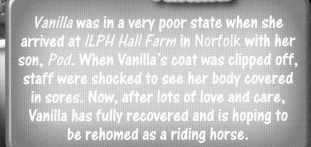

Vanilla

Vanilla was in a very poor state when she arrived at *ILPH Hall Farm* in Norfolk with her son, *Pod*. When Vanilla's coat was clipped off, staff were shocked to see her body covered in sores. Now, after lots of love and care, Vanilla has fully recovered and is hoping to be rehomed as a riding horse.

How You Can Help!

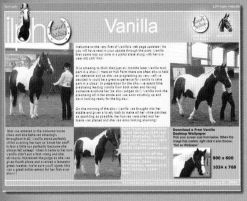

If you would like to rehome a horse or pony from the ILPH, visit the ILPH loan scheme pages at www.ilph.org/hls and if you see one you like, ask an adult to fill in the online form. Horses are rehomed on a loan basis and are checked regularly by an ILPH Field Officer.

You can also adopt a horse from ILPH. For £5 a month, adopters receive a welcome pack including a fab colour photo and badge and updates throughout the year on the horse they have adopted. T-shirts are available on request for fundraisers.

For more info on any of the horses at ILPH Farms visit www.ilphrangers.org or telephone 01953 497209.

ILPH PROTECTING HORSES WORLDWIDE

how to draw... kitten

Learn how to draw the cutest kitten and sweetest pup with these simple instructions - just grab a pencil!

1
Using a pencil, draw an oval shape on its side and then draw another shape round it as shown.

2 Under the first shapes you've drawn, add another 2 ovals like this.

3 Next, draw a couple of triangle ears on the top and a tail at the back. Rub out the lines between the bottom two ovals.

4 Draw a nose and a neck. Next, draw 3 circles as shown to make the kitten's paws.

5 Add the legs coming from the paws at the front and the back leg as shown.

6 Next, add some whiskers, eyes, a smiley face, a collar and lines to mark the back and front of the ears. Also, rub out the lines where the back paw joins the back leg.

7 Colour!

PUPPY

1 Draw 3 oval shapes as shown. Make sure the bottom one is bigger.

2 Rub out the lines that join the 2 smaller ovals.

3 Now, add another oval for the ear and 4 little circles for the puppy's paws.

4 Rub out the lines on the ear where it joins the head and the body as shown. Also rub out the lines where the 4 circles cross each other.

5 Now draw in the legs and add a nose, eye and mouth. Don't forget his waggy tail!

6 Rub out the lines where the legs join the body and draw on a spotty pattern.

7 Colour!

So Cute!

Aren't these the cutest pics caught on camera?

smile!

just hangin' around!

peek-a-boo

z z z z

50

a–z of best friends

It's what friendship's all about!

a Having friends is awesome!

b Every girl needs a bezzie buddy!

c Chocolate, cakes 'n' cookies, clothes and chat – all fun things to share with your pals!

d Dancing – meet up and make up some routines to your fave tunes.

e Email – yet another great way to talk to your bfs!

f Forever – it's how long we want our friendships to last!

g Best friends always have the best gossip!

h Happy! It's how friends make us feel.

i Include everyone in any invites – it's no fun being left out.

j Hanging out and sharing jokes are what bezzies do best!

k Always be kind to your pals.

l You'll never be lonely when you've got friends.

m Make up a memory book of fun things you've done with your mates Stick in your funniest photos and get everyone to write something in it

n It's lovely to have old friends but it's great fun to make new ones too!

o Need to look fabulous? Swap and share with your bfs and get a new outfit without spending a penny!

p A problem shared is a problem halved. Make sure you're always there for each other.

q You can't be friends with someone 100% of the time, so don't worry too much if you've quarrelled.

r Just resolve to fix any fights before they drag on too long and your friendship will be good as new.

s Shopping, sharing and secrets – it's what best buds are for!

t A best friend is someone you can trust. She'll keep your secrets safe forever.

u A best friend will understand if you feel unhappy.

v Valuable – a great pal is worth her weight in gold!

w Weekends are the best time to catch up with your pals and have fun together.

x Xtra-special – send your mate a text or buy her a big bar of choccy to show how much she means to you.

y Get together with your buds and yap till you're yawning.

z Zzzz! Sleepovers with your bezzies are so much fun

fit for fun!

Jumping, running, playing and spending time with you are a few of a dog's favourite things - so why not take your pet along to agility training? This is like keep fit and obedience classes for dogs and they love it! Check out your local area for a club. We popped into one in Eastbourne when the dogs and their owners were warming up. Even the fittest doggies may use muscles they've not used before!

Danielle tells Riley what she wants him to do. It's important to use different voices for commands and praise.

Now she holds a treat to help tempt him up the ramp.

Meanwhile, Gemma tries to get Roscoe's attention but he'd love to join in the fun with the other dogs. He's just a puppy and can't start classes until he's a year old. Aaw!

Peekaboo!

Now Danielle is telling her other dog, DD, what she'd like her to do. All dogs need to respond and understand basic commands.

Here, Danielle is teaching DD a new activity. It will take lots of time and patience with regular practice but DD will learn it at her own speed.

In and out...

Here I come...

Agility training teaches your dog to respond to you as quickly as possible and makes you and your dog a top team! Always remember, a confident, obedient dog is a happy dog!

ANIMAL boxes

You might need a little help folding and glueing these cute boxes but they're worth the effort!

You'll Need:

★ Tracing paper
★ Scissors
★ Glue
★ Sheets of thin coloured card
★ Colouring pens and extra scraps of card to decorate

1. Trace the **TOP** and **BASE** templates on to card.

2. Cut around the outside of the templates

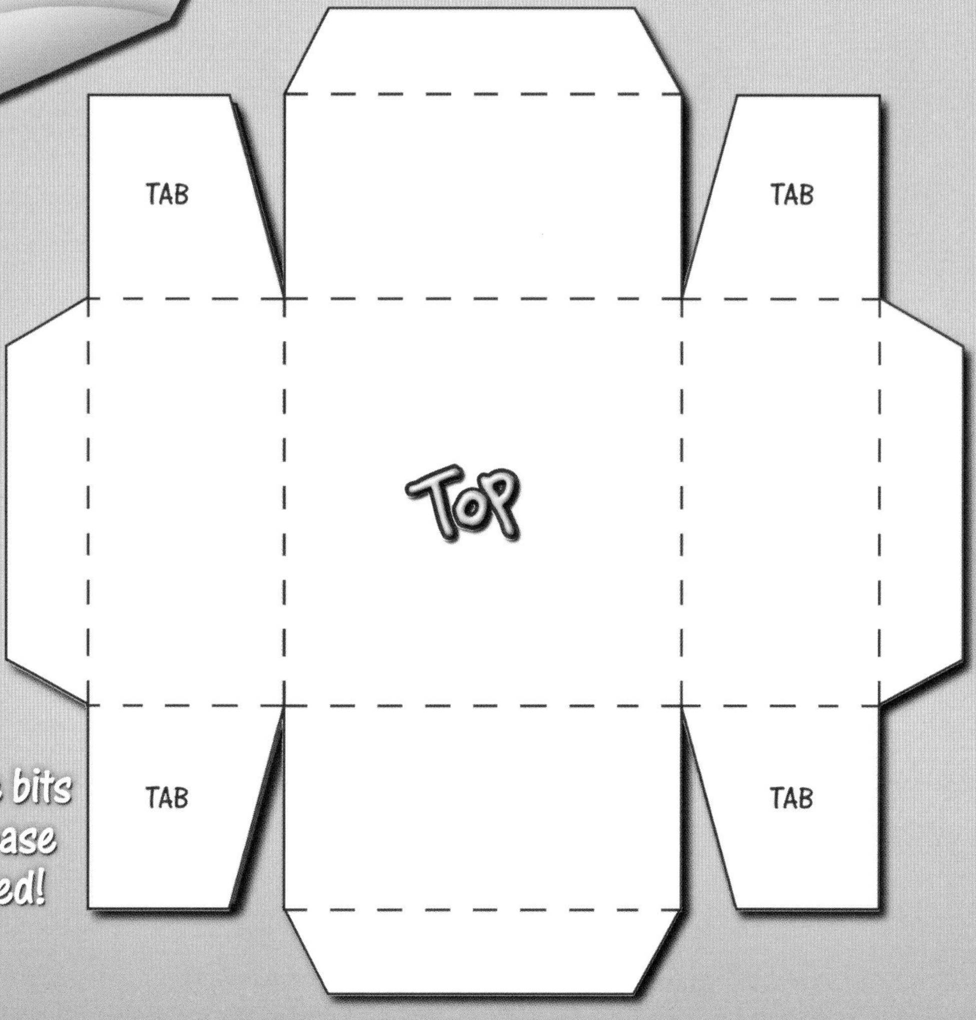

3. Now, fold along the dotted lines on the **BASE**. If you ask an adult to lightly score along these with scissors first, they'll be easier to fold. Fold the **TABS** in first, and glue carefully to sides. Next, fold the outer side bits in and glue these. The base of your box is now finished!

TAB

TAB

TOP

TAB

TAB

4. Now, fold along the dotted lines on the **TOP** and glue the tabs and sides in as before. Your box is ready to decorate!

5. Why not snip out ear, nose and tail shapes from coloured card? Or, simply draw on funny faces!

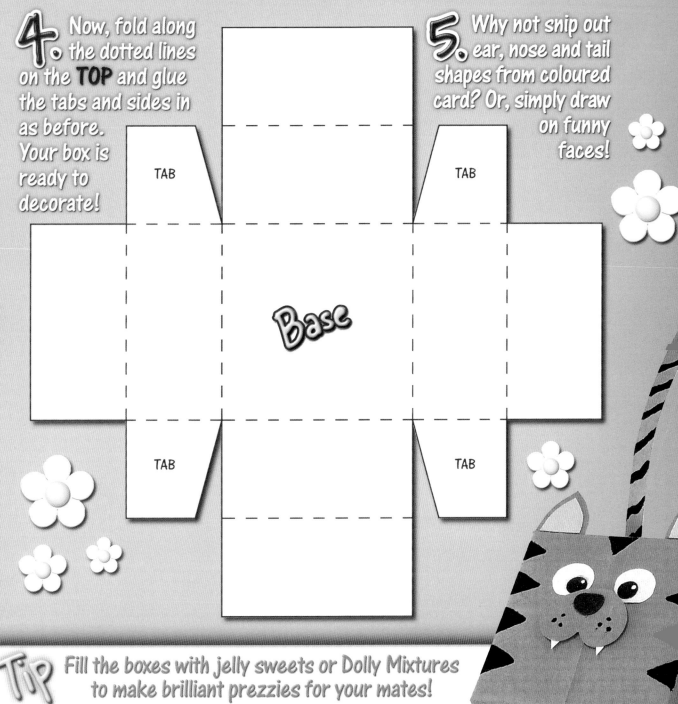

TAB

TAB

Base

TAB

TAB

Tip Fill the boxes with jelly sweets or Dolly Mixtures to make brilliant prezzies for your mates!

What's the best thing about winter?

What do you love most about winter? Follow the flow and find out what winter means to you!

Start
You love being outdoors?

Get Sporty!
You can't wait for it to start snowing so you can do winter sports – they're loads of fun!

Music Magic
You love it when all the shops start playing Christmas songs. You just can't help singing along!

Y

N

N

Y

N

Y

N

Y

N

N

Y

N

N

Y

Y

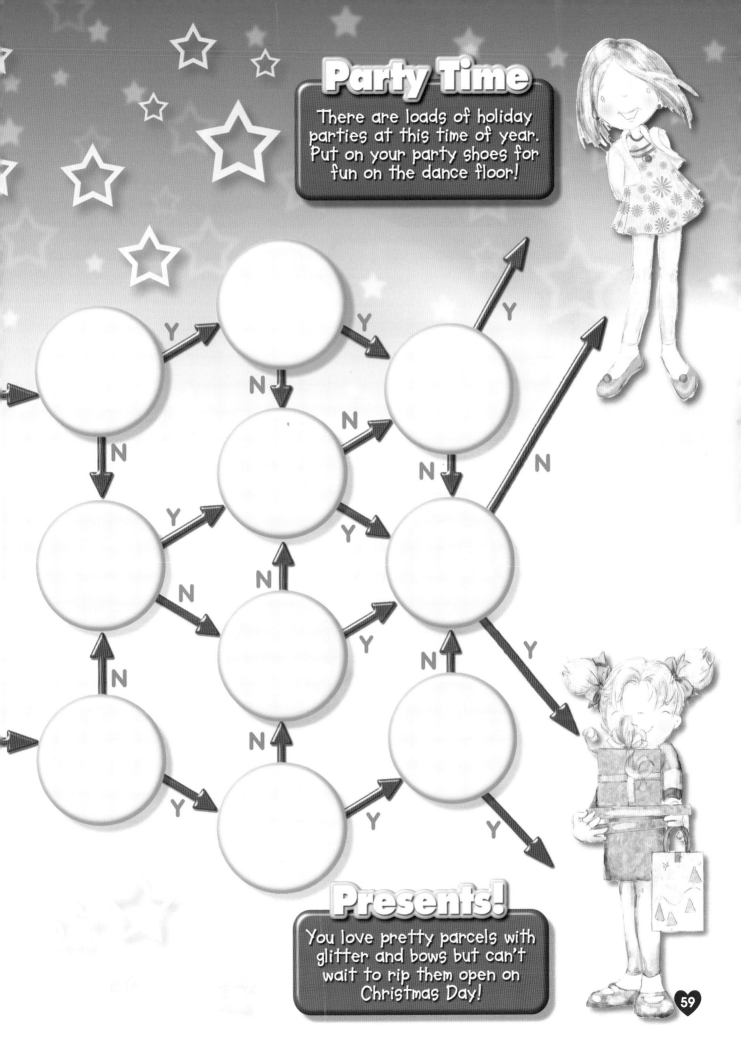

Party Time

There are loads of holiday parties at this time of year. Put on your party shoes for fun on the dance floor!

Presents!

You love pretty parcels with glitter and bows but can't wait to rip them open on Christmas Day!

White Out!

With their white fur and feathers these creatures blend in well with their snowy homes.

seal pup

Seal pups are born on ice floes around the chilly Arctic Ocean from late February to March.

Although well known for their snowy white fur, pups are actually born with yellow fur and are called Yellowbacks. However, after a few days, the yellow fur turns white.

Seal pups are very quick learners and will start to swim and feed all by themselves at about four weeks old.

arctic fox

The fur of the Arctic Fox is only white in winter so that it can stay hidden against the snow. When the snow melts, its fur turns a grey-brown colour to blend in with the rocks.

Arctic Foxes keep cosy in the coldest winter nights by burying their faces in their long, bushy tails.

snowshoe hare

Like the Arctic Fox, Snowshoe Hares change colour with the seasons. They are brown in summer and white, except for black ear tips, in winter.

Hares have powerful back legs and feet to help them travel quickly across the snow, so they can outrun their enemies.

61

Snowy Owl

Snowy Owls live alone in the frozen Arctic tundra. Another name for the Snowy Owl is the Ghost Owl as their white feathers make them almost invisible against the snow.

They are covered in cosy, fluffy feathers, even on their legs and feet! Snowy Owls are unable to move their eyes, so they spin their heads instead.

Unusually females are larger than the males and although they hoot like other owls, they are silent in winter.

polar bear

Polar Bears are the world's largest bears and are found in the frozen Arctic. Females can weigh more than 300kg and males may be twice that size. Although they look pure white, their skin is black.

They are strong swimmers and spend most of their time in the icy sea looking for food. On land, rough pads on their furry paws give them grip to walk on the ice.

Male Polar Bears are active all year, but females build snow dens and hibernate in the winter. Mums give birth in the den and come out with their cubs in spring.

63

purr-fectly happy!

Cats love to be played with every day but some cat toys are really expensive! Follow our 10 top tips to keep your fave feline happy without spending too much pocket money!

1 Ask Mum's permission to clear one of the shelves in your house for your cat to jump on and perch - it's much cheaper than buying a cat tree from a store!

2 Toss crumpled paper or plastic tops from milk cartons. Teach kitty to fetch!

3 Throw ping pong balls in the bathtub.

4 Slide straws or ice cubes across the floor.

5 Leave out cardboard boxes and brown paper bags for kitty to hide in.

6 Ask Dad for some spare rope and hang it somewhere safe for your pet to climb. Make sure it's kept well away from Mum's fave ornaments!

7 Stuff a sock with catnip and cotton balls.

8 Put the telly on to Animal Planet or leave a CD playing while you're away. It'll keep her company.

9 Brush your cat at least twice a week. She'll love the attention from you and regular brushing will help keep the cat hair off the couch.

10 Snuggle up in front of the TV together and reward yourselves with your fave treats!

Kat's Life!

We cats love summer. But sometimes getting peace to lie in the sun can be a bit of a problem!

Take one lovely sunny day last week . . .

I thought I'd found the very spot!

Libby's mum appeared —

Sorry, Kat, but I must water the garden.

If there's one thing cats hate, It's getting wet!

Let's hope I have more luck in this part of the garden!

Then Libby and her friends turned up —

I'm going to ask Mum to do a barbie.

Cool! I'm starving!

And so —

That smells delicious!

It won't be long.

But while the girls were enjoying themselves . . .

But outside . . .

I don't like the look of those black clouds.

And moments later . . .

Come on, girls, inside.

Of course, they made so much noise, I woke up . . .

Come on, Kat. Here's a piece of chicken for you

Right! That's it! Smoked out! Inside for me!

Peace at last!

Just in time! It's pouring with rain!

I know! We'll have an indoor picnic.

How about putting on some music, Libby?

Well, at least the food was good!

Now, if you don't mind, I have rather a lot of sleep to catch up on!

SWEET-O-KU!

It's the cutest sudoku ever! Can you correctly fit these fluffy cuddlies into the grid? Every row, column and mini-grid must contain one picture of each of them.

answers

rescued!

Registered charity no.219099

The **RSPCA** helps lots of animals who are in danger or need a new home. This is one of their more unusual rescue stories!

A woman and her daughter were driving along a country road near Capernwray, a village in Lancashire. They spotted something very different on the grass at the side of the road. When they stopped the car to have a look they discovered it was a seal pup!

They didn't have the phone number for the RSPCA but didn't want to leave him where he was, so they wrapped him up and put him in the boot of their car. They took him to a nearby farm and the little seal was put into a calf stall until the RSPCA arrived.

The RSPCA thought that the little seal pup had swum up a river and then waddled across the countryside. They took him to one of their Wildlife Centres where staff decided to call him Ghost because his big, black eyes were so haunting.

Ghost was released back into the sea as soon as possible as he was healthy and eating them out of herring!

Hopefully **Ghost** won't be visiting the countryside again any time soon!

To find out more about the **RSPCA** and the work they do log on to **www.rspca.org.uk**

69